Uncle Harold's
Maxwell House Haggadah

Uncle Harold's Maxwell House Haggadah

Danny Caine

Etchings Press
Indianapolis, Indiana

2017

Copyright© 2017 by Danny Caine

This publication is made possible by funding provided by the Shaheen College of Arts and Sciences and the English Department of the University of Indianapolis. Special thanks to IngramSpark and to those students who judged, edited, designed, and published this chapbook: Josie Seach, Courtney Loshe, and Matthew Byrd.

UNIVERSITY *of* INDIANAPOLIS.

Published by Etchings Press
1400 E. Hanna Avenue
Indianapolis, Indiana 46227
All rights reserved

etchings.uindy.edu
www.uindy.edu/cas/english

Printed by IngramSpark
ingramspark.com

Published in the United States of America

ISBN 978-0-9988976-8-4

23 22 21 20 19 18   3 4 5
Third Printing, June 2019

"The Four Sons and One God-Forbid Future Daughter In Law" appeared in *Mid-American Review*. "Why I Didn't Ask My Wife to Convert" appeared in *The Legendary*.

Table of Contents

Kadesh	1
We Raise the First Glass and Say	2
SEDER CHECKLIST	3
The Inflatable Matzoh Ball of Affliction	4
Mitzvah Aleinu L'saper Biytziyat Mitzrayim	5
Maggid	7
We Raise the Second Glass and Say	8
The Seven Plagues I Could Find	9
The Four Sons and One God-Forbid Future Daughter-in-Law	10
We Begin to Answer, or Maybe Not	11
Separate Seders: The Exodus of Grandpa	13
Shulchan Orech	15
The Language We Grieve in is Trays	16
Creed	17
The Bagelox Boy Becomes a Man	19
Barech	21
We Raise the Third Glass and Say	22
The Four Sons in Exodus	23
The Sedermeister's Steps to Selling Your House	24
The Fifth Question	25
Hallel	26
We Raise the Fourth Glass and Say	27
The Wicked Son Prepares to Find the Afikomen	28
Dayenu	29
Epilogue: Why I Didn't Ask My Wife to Convert	31

Kadesh

[We say the Kiddush]
[First glass of wine]

We Raise the First Glass and Say

Let all who are hungry come and eat. Let all who are in need come and celebrate Passover. This year we are here, next year in Jerusalem and *this year* Maxwell House hired an ad agency to convince a rabbi to declare coffee Kosher For Passover and *this year* Maxwell House started giving away Haggadahs with cans of coffee and *this year* I actually tried to keep Kosher and ate Matzoh Pizza with pepperoni every night.

This year Aunt Lisa bought the Rite Lite® Ten Plagues Toy Kit and *this year* Uncle Harold downloaded the Passover PowerPoint and *this year* Uncle Harold and Aunt Lisa screamed at each other in the living room and *this year* Grandma gave everyone only two ice cubes and this year we never forget: only two ice cubes.

This year Grandpa married the much-younger shiksa and *this year* Grandpa didn't show up and *this year* Uncle Harold became Sedermeister and *this year* Grandpa had a fall and some heart stuff and so began his apology tour and so began his return.

This year we got new Haggadahs and *this year* we tread lightly in the house because Aunt Lisa died there and *this year* we did the toy plagues anyway and this year Uncle Harold introduced us to his new girlfriend and *this year* Uncle Harold sold his house.

This year I started writing poems about us and *this year* we took away Grandma's car and *this year* grandma died and this year one of the grand-children had children and this year Uncle Harold became Grandfather Harold and *this year* I moved to Kansas and *this year* I didn't go to the Seder and *this year we are here, next year in Jerusalem*, or at least Cleveland, at least Uncle Harold's folding chairs.

SEDER CHECKLIST

Holiday Candles
One bottle Wine
> *Eh, bring a good one*
> *Eh, bring a liter of Manischevitz too*

Seder Plate
Cup for Elijah
> *Don't forget the Rite Lite® Ten Plagues Toy Kit*

Three matzot, covered
A plate of pickles, hidden
> *for these cousins, pickles are like money*

Salt water for dipping
Cup, basin, towel for washing
> *Eh, what's the difference if I use the sink*

At least one shiksa girlfriend
Haggadah for each person
> *even the girlfriend*

Wine cup for each person
> *except the two youngest cousins*
> *and the girlfriend*

Optional:

Matzoh of Hope
> *Harold? What on earth is a Matzoh of Hope?*

Afikomen bag
Money for Afikomen
Empty plate to remember the homeless
Empty plate to remember those in the diaspora of death
Empty plate to remember those in the diaspora of *divorce*
Empty plates to remember the 4 sons who moved away
> *Where are we gonna put all these empty plates?*

The Inflatable Matzoh Ball of Affliction

Wherefore is this night distinguished from all
other nights? Any other night we may eat
either leavened or unleavened bread, but on this night only
> *Wavy Lay's Kosher for Passover.*

and our children and our children's children
> will have Bissli Pizza Flavor Party Snack
> and Manischevitz Fruity Magic Loops Cereal.

because it is written: in the Maxwell House Haggadah—

This is the bread of affliction
> and the Passover Coke of affliction,
> and the Rite Lite Inflatable Matzoh Ball of affliction,
> and the Manischevitz Milk Chocolate Lollycones
> > of affliction.

Baruch Atah Adonai, Eloheinu Melech haolam, Borei p'ri
  Manischevitz

Blessed art thou, O Lord, our God, who createst
> Manischevitz American Concord Grape
> > Specially Sweetened
> > > Containing Not Less than 51% Concord Wine—
> > > and Kedem Grape Juice for the shiksa girlfriend.

Mitzvah Aleinu L'saper Biytziyat Mitzrayim.

[It is a commandment upon us to tell of the exodus from Egypt]

Mitzvah aleinu not l'saper Biytziyat Grandpa
>[We do not tell of Grandpa's exodus]
>[Uncle Harold is Sedermeister now]
>[the divorce already gave Grandma one stroke]

Mitzvah
>[barks at something in the backyard]

Uncle Harold
>[yells at Mitzvah]
>[rises to wash his hands]

Ur'Chatz
>[we are supposed to wash our hands too]
>[only Uncle Harold does]

L'Hadlik ner Shel Yom Tov
>[the candles are lit]
>[did I miss the blessing?]
>[do we even do that one?]

Aleinu to recline in our chairs
>[only Uncle Harold does]
>[the wicked son does too]
>[his is a slouching adolescence]

Aleinu
>[to spill the manischevitz on the white lace]

Mitzvah Aleinu L'saper
> [the Seder must run 30 minutes]
> [no more, no less]
> [even Grandpa knew this]
> [in Uncle Harold's Maxwell House Haggadah]
> [you can still see the highlights]

Mitzvah Aleinu L'saper
> [we take turns reading]
> [visitors too]
> [even the girlfriend]
> [she can read the parts with the Hebrew names]
> [listen to her trip on Gamliel, Eliazar, Yocheved]

Maggid

[we tell the story of Passover]
[we tell the story of Exodus]
[second glass of wine]

We Raise the Second Glass and Say

We praise you, Adonai our God, Ruler of the Universe,
Who has freed us and our ancestors from Egypt and brought us
    to Cleveland

this night to eat matzoh and maror. Adonai,
our God and God of our ancestors, help us celebrate
future holidays
    in Cleveland and Cleveland alone
    or Jerusalem, I guess
    but not New York
    or Kansas
    or Columbus
    or Las Vegas.

Adonai our God Help us celebrate future holidays
and festivals in peace and in joy
    and not in diminishing numbers—

Then we will thank you with a new song,
l'chayim.

The Seven Plagues I Could Find

When we recall these plagues, we remove a toy, each a symbol of joy, from our Rite Lite Ten Plagues Kit®, because the deliverance of our people from the hands of the Egyptians was 25% off last year. Together, let us recall the Ten Plagues against Egypt:

The red shotglass that says "blood,"	דָּם
the small plastic frog,	צְפַרְדֵּעַ
the plastic praying mantis,	כִּנִּים
I coulda sworn there was a lion in here—is that Beasts?	עָרוֹב
the slide-the-squares puzzle of a verklempt cow,	דֶּבֶר
the sticky gummyhand with white spots,	שְׁחִין
the red and white bouncyball,	בָּרָד
is this a Lice or a Locust?	אַרְבֶּה
I couldn't find Darkness, which figures,	חֹשֶׁךְ
and I lost the First Born, too, but then again	מַכַּת בְּכוֹרוֹת

    so did the Egyptians.

The Four Sons and One God-Forbid Future Daughter-In-Law

What says the wise son? He asks: "What are these testimonies, statues, and judgments which the Eternal, our God hath commanded you?" Then thou shalt instruct him in the laws of the Passover, that a good Seder runs max 30 minutes and that, when it is his turn to be Sedermister, if Uncle Harold should run off with a shiksa half his age like his father before him, he shalt never deviate from the highlighted parts.

What says the simple son? He asks: "What is this?" Then thou shalt tell him: "What do you mean, *what is this*? It's Passover. Don't be a putz."

What says the wicked son? He asks: "What mean you by taking away my cell phone when dad can keep his?" Then thou shalt tell him: "dad is a goy, so he can play Angry Birds during Seder."

For he who hath no capacity to inquire thou must begin the narration as it is said: "go in the other room and watch the Indians."

And what says the wise son's shiksa girlfriend? She asks: "What mean you by this service?" By the word "you," it is clear that she doth not include herself because she's a Lutheran and is taking the wise son to Easter this Sunday, and therefore was never one of us to begin with. It is therefore proper to retort upon her by saying, "It's a long story."

We Begin To Answer, Or Maybe Not

We cousins are four men—
wise, wicked, simple,
and cannot ask a question.
There is one woman—

Allison: we cousins are five.
But the Haggadah speaks
only of sons. One cousin son
now has twin baby boys—

are they sons 5 and 6?
Wise, simple, wicked,
cannot answer a question,
and two more who cannot do

much but spit up and kvetch?
(In that way they pick up
Grandma's work). Or are they sons
one and two, a new generation

of Afikomen scavengers?
Where did Harold hide
the Afiko-women?
My brother and I are

Caines. not able to call
ourselves Wassermen
like everyone else.
Nobody calls himself

or herself a Wasserwoman,
But again, as it is written
on tombstones and Bar Mitzvah
kipahs and receipts taped to deli trays:

We are Wassermen. Except
the Caines. In the Book
Cain is the wicked one, so
it must still be us.

Wise is the one who made
Jewish twin babies. Wicked
are the ones who bring
goyim ladies to Seder.

Wicked are the ones who heartbreak
mothers by leaving Cleveland.

Separate Seders:
The Exodus of Grandpa

He had a boat and a condo

He had a Lexus

He had a divorce.

Grandma had a stroke.

We tried to have a Seder

He wouldn't talk to her

"tell your mother to pass the pickles"

One year Grandpa didn't show up.

Grandpa tried to come into the family room

Rabbi Matt took him by the elbow,

and then he didn't.

and he had a Chrysler.

The younger cousins still don't know why.

The cousins can guess why.

with both of them anyway.

except to look at Uncle Harold and say

we tried separate seders.

One year much later Grandma died.

at the Funeral home.

led him away.

Shulcan Orech

[we eat the festive meal]

The Language We Grieve in is Trays

What do you mean I don't like lox of course I like lox. Creamed herring maybe not, but lox, yes. A cookie tray? You shouldn't have. Here, put this in the garage with the other 7. Did grandma like creamed herring? Mom preferred gefilte fish. Did you know gefilte fish is made of Asian Carp? It can't be. I heard on NPR you can't eat Asian Carp. A cookie tray? You shouldn't have. Here put this in the garage with the other 8. Kevin—the Catholic one!—looked up why we sit on short chairs. It's to sit closer to the deceased but I think that's gross. Yeah plus mom's in heaven anyway. Jack's does a good dairy tray, you know? For $300 they better. $300? Mom didn't make this cheap. Are you sure you don't want to take cookies back to Kansas? A cookie tray? You shouldn't have. Here put this in the garage with the other 9. Too bad these cookies aren't kosher for Passover. Maybe Danny will take some back to Kansas. Are you writing down who brought what? Aunt Lynn's friend Rickie sent a tray. Uncle Mike's poker friends sent a tray. Alan's friend George sent a tray. Grandma's boyfriend's daughter sent a tray. Aunt Lynn's Sunday school teacher colleagues sent a tray. Judy's officemates sent a tray. They're from a small bakery in Hudson. I like to support small business, especially ones owned by women. These Giant Eagle sugar cookies are killer. Are you sure you don't want to take some back to Kansas?

Creed

with a small debt to Ezra Koenig

We are not Reform not Reconstructionist
Not Hasidic Not Orthodox Not Ultra-Orthodox
Not Conservative Not Conservadox:

we are The Bagelox Jews.

We believe in the food from the countries
where they tried to kill our grandparents

and we will fight
       with our wallets
              to preserve the places
                      that serve it.

May H&H Bagels Rest in Peace.
May Essa Bagel soldier on.

We can name the top three Bagels
the top three bowls of Matzoh Ball Soup
and the top three Corned Beef Sandwiches
in Cleveland, New York, Chicago, and LA.

In Cleveland: Corkey's for soup
Slyman's for Corned Beef,
Bialys for bagels and Jack's
for Shiva trays.

We believe our aunt's soup
is better than your aunt's soup.

We are not sure what we believe
about Israel--we watched Zionist
VHS in Sunday School but we read
about colonialism and genocide
at tiny colleges in the Midwest.

There are no pro-IDF sermons
in our halls, but there may be

a laminated poster of the Dome of the Rock
in our second-favorite Falafel shop
on the Upper West Side.

We are not sure what we believe
about God, but we're not atheists—
we are no unbelievers.

We believe in the exodus
God fed the Jews.

We believe in the diaspora
God feeds the Jews.

Putting the "Bar" in "Bar Mitzvah:" The Bagelox Boy Becomes a Man

Only after your cousin Jeff has taken
you to your first bar—

a tin-ceiling narrow brick Brooklyn place
called Pencil Factory, across from an old
Pencil Factory—

only after the bartender has called you
forward   [Aliyah]

to recite the words Jeff taught you
to say   [Parshah] *Jameson and Ginger*

only after   [haftarah] *beer please*
                  [haftarah] *beer please*
                  [haftarah] *white Russian please*

only after you go to the apartment
behind the store where Jeff's stylish
friends sell sarongs and incense
              [reception]

only after you have puffed and passed
              [borei prei hagafen]

only after you have passed out in the cab
to the surreal static litany of the dispatcher
              [Kaddish]

only after you have woken up on Jeff's
expensive midcentury couch with flames
in your forehead
                [Ad'Vil]

can you go to Second Avenue Deli and order
                [Aliyah]
Matzoh Ball Soup

only after you've slurped the soup
                [maggid]
can you rest your head on the cool table

trying not to spit up when the waiter
brings the Corned Beef on Rye
                [hamotzi]

only after you've coughed down half
the sandwich can you wrap it in a napkin

and only after you've winced into the sun
can you descend to the sweaty L train

can you become ravenous finally
and eat that half sandwich in two
bites and become a [Wasser]man
                [bar mitzvah]

Barech

[we say the blessing after the meal]
[third glass of wine]
[welcome Elijah the prophet]

We Raise the Third Glass and Say

This cup is for Eliyahu Hanavi, Elijah the Prophet. We open our front door to greet our honored guest and invite him to join our seder. We pray that he will return to us bringing a time of peace and freedom.

This cup is for cousin Jeff, who moved to NYC to become an architect and marry a pretty Jewish girl from Hudson and buy a cute purebred and a weekend house upstate. We open our front door to greet him and invite him to join our Seder. We pray that he will return to us, even though he probably won't.

And *this c*up is for Danny, who married a gentile and moved to Kansas to write poems about us even though he won't let us read them. Even though you can't get a health-insurance pension-plan job with an MFA. We open our front door to greet him and invite him to join our Seder. We pray that he will return to us, even though he probably won't.

And *this* cup is for Grandma, who died months before becoming a great Grandma. We open our front door to greet her and invite her to join our Seder. We pray that she will return to us, even though she probably won't. If she does, we pray that she remembers her meshuggah hearing aids. And *this* cup is for Cousin Alan, and his twins at their first Seder. We open our front door to greet our honored guests, to welcome the ones who actually showed up.

Let us call Uncle Harold Grandfather Harold for the first time. Let us thank God for the most precious of all his gifts: Jewish grandchildren. New Wassermen. Let us add more, subtract less. May the other cousins take a ferkakta hint.

The Four Sons in Exodus

Months ago my brother told me he's applying for a job
at a trendy online company that's hellbent on rebuilding
the shell of Downtown Las Vegas. I imagined brightly
painted walls. A climbing wall. Bosses on Segways. No,
he hadn't told mom yet. Yes, he was aware it would break
her. We were at the Annex, the only bar near our parents'
house. We were home for grandma's funeral. This was
supposed to be the one chance we had to relax on my
quick trip home. But then again he was supposed to be
the One That Stayed Home. Neither Moses nor Aaron
made it to the promised land. Their lives were diaspora.
Grandpa Wasserman went from Minsk to Montreal to
Cleveland and stayed there eating Corky & Lenny's
and Bialys from Heaven until all four sons left. Wise
simple wicked cannot ask a question. New York Kansas
Columbus and now Las Vegas. Maybe not in that order.
Columbus we'll take because he made new Wassermen.
At least Allison, our generation's Wasserwoman, stayed.

Uncle Harold's חַי: The Sedermeister's Steps to Selling Your House

1. Convert the Methodist you marry, Raise your son in the tribe
2. When your parents divorce, it is your turn to be Sedermeister
3. Create the Passover Powerpoint
4. Smile while your son marries a Catholic
5. Smile at your sister's surprise baptism
6. Smile as your daughter-in-law converts
7. Sit Shiva for your wife
8. A Jack's dairy tray for the mourners
9. Keep the house on the market for
10. Months and months with no leads
11. Ask your newly Catholic sister which Saint sells houses
12. Bury The St. Joseph Home Seller Kit® head toward the house
13. Accept the bid
14. Move your mom into a home and another kind of home
15. Is it relief you feel when she dies, that it was pretty quick?
16. A Jack's dairy tray for the mourners
17. *Keep St. Joseph in a place of honor in your new home*
18. Next to the Menorah

The Fifth Question

"Do you have a fifth question about the Seder that you would like to ask?"

Why doesn't cousin Alan like Uncle Harold's
new girlfriend? Why did all our sons move away
but our daughter stayed? Who ate all the pickles
already? Does Alan still keep Playboys under his bed?
Is Maror the apple stuff or the horseradish? When
does one of the cousins host the seder? When can
you come home and meet the twins? When is Jeff
gonna have kids? Matt, are you seeing anyone?
Allison, are you seeing anyone? Danny, when are
you gonna have kids? Are your kids gonna be Jewish?
Isn't killing the first born a bit harsh? Why does
the New York cousin like the Cavs and the Columbus
cousin like the Yankees? What's the score of the Indians
Yankees game? What does it look like when a mountain
skips like a ram? Why are all the cousins together only
at funerals? Why does a coffee corporation sponsor
Passover? Why hasn't Danny shown us his poems?

Hallel

[we sing songs of praise]
[fourth glass of wine]

We Raise the Fourth Glass and Say

all other nights we drink as many
glasses of wine as we wish;
tonight it is a commandment unto us
to drink four—

and Aunt Lynn maybe two as her
digestion is bad enough to begin with—

and mom none, as the fruit of the vine
giveth her the migraine.

On this night thou shalt give
Cousin Matt the stink eye
as he pours forth too much
into his third glass.

On this night I suppose you can
give her some fruit of the vine
since she's the shiksa
wife now.

And on this night thou shalt, all of you
after dessert lose interest in the Seder
and rise to wash the dishes—
to see if the Indians are winning—
to play fetch with Mitzvah—

and thus shalt thou leave Uncle Harold
to pray and drink the fourth glass alone.

The Wicked Son Prepares To Find the Afikomen

Shake the Halleluyah Tambourine® and bust
out the Matzah Crumb Sweeper® because
it's Afiokoman time, schmucks.

If someone else cashes in on Uncle Harold's
cold hard shekels, I will slap them with mom's Matzah
Pattern Printed Oven Mitt®. Don't think I'm kidding—

I'm packing a Star of David Swiss Army Knife® and I
am NOT afraid to use it. With last year's Afikoman
I bought a book called *But He Was Good To His Mother*:

The Lives and Crimes of Jewish Gangsters, and I've learned
A lot. Plus, the last thing I see before I go to bed
is my IDF Kfir C7 Fighter Jet Die Cast Model.

Call me the wicked son but since I've been able to walk
I've been 8 for 8 on the Pesach payday, even if it meant
some cousins got a Matzah Pattern Kipah® stuffed

down their ferkakta throats. I'm unstoppable like
the Waterskiing Rabbis framed on Uncle Harold's
bathroom wall. I'm plucky and determined

like Moses or Aaron or Judah Maccabe. Let me answer
your four questions right here, right now: our ancestors
schlepped outta Egypt before they could bake bread,

so now we get *paid* at the end of every Seder, but only
if we're fast and only if we're ruthless. No, *mom*, I will not
stop plotzing. Seder's over, festive meal is done,
it's time to part the Red Sea, it's time to run.

Dayenu

If He had executed judgment upon their gods, and had not slain their first-born *Dayenu*

If He had slain their first-born, and had not bestowed their wealth on us *Dayenu*

If He had given us their wealth, and had not divided the sea for us *Dayenu*

If He had divided the sea for us, and had not ensured that the turkey didn't dry out *Dayenu*

If He had kept the turkey moist, and had not brought together, like, three of the cousins this year *Dayenu*

If He had brought Allison Matt and Alan, and had not converted Alan's wife *Dayenu*

If He had made Alan's wife one of us and not borne her twins *Dayenu*

If He had given us the twins, and had not given us the Passover Powerpoint *Dayenu*

If he had given us the Passover Powerpoint and not the Rite Lite® Ten Plagues Kit *Dayenu*

If he had bestowed the fun plagues upon us and had not wrapped things up in time for the 7th inning, *Dayenu*

For all these—alone and together—we say,

Dayenu

Amen

Epilogue: Why I Didn't Ask My Wife to Convert

When my mom at 54 stood before St. Dominic's
with my dad, when my brother and I watched
from the seats as Father Tom did his thing
with the water, you could say I was Pewish.

I'm still Pewish some Sundays when I squeeze
out of the way so the believers can sway by to take
the wine and the biscuit. Now my family really is
Half Jewish: kids yes, parents no. O, 'Half Jewish,'

you eternal answer to December questions. My Jewish side
craves bagels and lox, the other loves lobster. Corned beef
swings both ways. My height is Jewish and my nose is not.
My diabetes will be Jewish; my wife will not.

In Hebrew school my class asked Morah Shifrah how
to convert to Judaism. She said hard work. We asked
how to convert *from* Judaism. She said you cannot.
Morah Shifrah I have broken your first commandment:

marry a Jewish girl. I see your point, though. I can
imagine the postwar promises of never again, of go forth
and multiply, of descendants and the grains of sand.
In every generation they rise up against us:

do you blame the shiksas this time, seducing all our mensches
into lives of Easter egg hunts and bacon cheese burgers?
Lock me up then, I'm guilty. But let me ask you: have you
been on the other end? Have you ever had a lover

tell you in bed you're going to hell? When you're raised in halves, you don't know which side will find what makes you whole. My wife didn't ask me to change a goddamn thing about my ferkakta self. I didn't ask her to convert.

Special Thanks

Thanks to Phil Metres and Megan Kaminski for the enthusiastic mentorship. Thanks to Paige Webb for being a good reader and a great friend. Thanks to Kara Caine for being my best friend and a constant source of support. Finally, huge thanks (and perhaps apologies) to the Wasserman family. You've always helped me remember that eating and laughing are part of being Jewish. This chapbook is dedicated to Natalie Wasserman and Sanford Wasserman.

Colophon

Body Text and Poem titles in Baskerville.
Cover set in Baskerville.

Danny Caine's poetry has appeared or is forthcoming in *Hobart*, *Mid-American Review*, *DIAGRAM*, *Minnesota Review*, *New Ohio Review* and other places. He is music editor for *At Length* and reviews books for *Los Angeles Review*. Hailing from Cleveland, he lives in Lawrence, Kansas, where he works at Raven Book Store. Find him online at dannycaine.com.

Etchings Press

Etchings Press is a student-run publisher at the University of Indianapolis. Each year, student editors choose the Whirling Prize, a post-publication award, in the fall and coordinate a publication contest for one poetry chapbook, one prose chapbook, and one novella in the spring. For more information, please visit etchings.uindy.edu.

Previous winners and publications

Poetry
2019: *As Lovers Always Do* by Marne Wilson
2018: *In the Herald of Improbable Misfortunes* by Robert Campbell
2017: *Uncle Harold's Maxwell House Haggadah* by Danny Caine
2016: *Some Animals* by Kelli Allen
2015: *Velocity of Slugs* by Joey Connelly
2014: *Action at a Distance* by Christopher Petruccelli

Prose
2019: *Dissenting Opinion from the Committee for the Beatitudes* by Marc J. Sheehan (fiction)
2018: *The Forsaken* by Chad V. Broughman (fiction)
2017: *Unravelings* by Sarah Cheshire (memoir)
2016: *Pathetic* by Shannon McLeod (essays)
2015: *Ologies* by Chelsea Biondolillo (essays)
2014: *Static: Stories* by Frederick Pelzer (fiction)

Novella
2019: *Savonne, Not Vonny* by Robin Lee Lovelace
2018: *Edge of the Known Bus Line* by James R. Gapinski
2017: *The Denialist's Almanac of American Plague and Pestilence* by Christopher Mohar
2016: *Followers* by Adam Fleming Petty

www.ingramcontent.com/pod-product-compliance
Lightning Source LLC
Chambersburg PA
CBHW070442010526
44118CB00014B/2159